Leaves to Stay

Kristen Dunn

I dedicate this book to my mom, Elizabeth, may she rest in peace.

Contents

The Game of Life

The skyline at night is so pretty
But it belongs to such a cold-hearted city
Says I have a chance
But I really don't
Says I will succeed
But I really won't
Builds me up every time
Rips out from under me what was mine
Chicago, I did nothing wrong
I played your rules
I sang along
Good memories fade til they are gone
I'll disappear with them
It won't be long
My life awaits in a different state
Each car ride is a future bound gate
Life's a game so I will play mine
By the time I win
I'll be where the sun shines
Builds me up every time
Rips out from under me what was mine
Chicago, I did nothing wrong
I played your rules
I sang along
Good memories fade til they are gone
I'll disappear with them
It won't be long

And so I stray

One step forward
Two steps back
Is this really where my life is at?
Sunny, warm, calm, and free
But then there is the moon's mystery…

The Middle of Chicago

The way the air sparkles
And the indigo trees around
Can you sit in the middle of Chicago?
Without hearing a sound?
You can say this city is pretty
Or you can say it's hell and crime
But can you sit in the middle of Chicago?
Casually stopping time?
Seagulls circle the air
Cars accelerate in the streets
Can you sit in the middle of Chicago?
Without your exhales deplete?
Construction on every corner
With the lake up ahead
Can you sit in the middle of Chicago?
And have that be your bed?
The breeze that sends shivers
And the cold metal bench
Can you sit in the middle of Chicago?
And let that loosen every clench?
Skyscrapers that tower
But from faraway look small
Can you sit in the middle of Chicago?
While watching yourself fall?
The slowly moving branches
On the deeply rooted trees
Can you sit in the middle of Chicago?
And find your missing piece?
Enveloped in the street lights

It will never get too dark
Can you sit in the middle of Chicago?
And say you have made your mark?

Heaven

Don't you dare dig me a hole
Don't you try to push me in
I have come way too far in this
To ever let you win
Yes, I was so depressed
No, I wasn't gonna survive
But my soul met my body
And now I am alive
I live in this heaven of mine
Don't try to break me and stop my shine
I already know that it's not my time
Let me be myself and I'll be fine
Yes, I was a destructive mess
I think I always was
I'll always have that side of me
That's what being a human does
I need to see the world
That's been a dream that I've had
To travel around the US
And never look back
I live in this heaven of mine
Don't try to break me and stop my shine
I already know that it's not my time
Let me be myself and I'll be fine

Mountains

I made it to the mountains
I think I really am free
There's so much out there to explore
There's so much out there to see
I didn't think I would get here
The probability was against me
But I'm here on these red rocks
I just accomplished victory
I will never be tied down
I will never stay in one place
I have so much I need to do
I have so much I need to face
I am a rose with petals unknown
With every new experience the less it matters
Let the petals fall and let them fly free
I am traveling with my soul
And that is all I need

Dangerous place

Colors shine so bright
When darkness surrounds
I'm running away
So I can never be found
When I try to fly high
I bury myself in the ground
I play my own music
I love my own sound
I sit in the sun
But walk under the moon
Can't ever go inside
It's always too soon
I get mad at myself
If I sleep past noon
I must be productive
Or else I lose my tune
When happy I shine bright
When sad I'm dark
But it was brightness
That brought me to the secret park
The light at the end of the tunnel
Was what caught my eye
But if the tunnel wasn't so dark
Would the light of been that bright?
They say beauty is pain
They say beauty is appeal
But what's so beautiful
About the things that I feel?
I go through many obstacles

While trying to heal
Situations so wild
Situations so real
Expand my mind
But stay planted on the ground
Reach for the stars
While to this earth I'm bound
As I climb up
I'm constantly falling down
I hate Chicago
I hate downtown
Fire burns
And water flows
I am a fire sign
A fire that grows
I have learned one thing
This poem is proof I know
That my mind is a dangerous place to be in alone

Growing

I'm growing old
I'm growing weak
I see it in my face
I hear it when I speak
I remember when I felt like I was at my peak
Flying so high and swept off my feet
The flying didn't last long
It was over as fast as it began
Fell to the ground with a shovel and started digging where I stand
All while telling myself this was never what I planned
So I kept digging and let others lend a hand
The farther I dug
The further from the light
There was no such thing as day
There was only night
Turned true friends away when they witnessed this sad sight
Trying to show them they were wrong and I'm the only one that's
right
Now I sit on a beach
The same beach I used to sit
And would write about happiness
And my journey for it
I'm here with people I met this year
Maybe they are my friends
Or maybe they are just using me til the day I end
I used to dream of mountains, sunshine, and trees
Those dreams went away
Once they became reality

Struggles

Stabbing pain
In my heart
I think it was that way to start
Restless struggles
Lay deep within
Fighting myself and trying to win

Losing stars

They say you measure
This life in years
What does that mean?
It's so unclear
They say you measure
Each month by the moon
I don't like that measurement
It fades away too soon
And all the pain
And all the tears
Falling to the ground
Just to end up right here
And all the eyes
And all the smiles
They lit up my heart
So it was all worth the while
Growing growing growing
Feeling good and strong
What took me down?
Where did I go wrong?
Refuse to be defeated
Taking back control
Just wish this power struggle
Didn't take its toll
And all the pain
And all the tears
Falling to the ground
Just to end up right here
And all the eyes

And all the smiles
They lit up my heart
So it was all worth the while
Look at me I have the world
Look at me I lost the stars
Look at me I'm searching for marbles
Look at me
It isn't hard
And all the pain
And all the tears
Falling to the ground
Just to end up right here
And all the eyes
And all the smiles
They lit up my heart
So it was all worth the while

Spiral

Dying when I wake up
No relief in sleep
Every morning is a hassle
Just to get on my feet
I wake up to a nightmare
I wake up to death
Every time I walk towards the light
My shadow takes a step
When I stand
My feet don't touch the ground
I am forever falling
The darkest spiral down
Stab me in my heart
Watch the anger flow away
They say the sun is shining
But I can't see the rays

The New Year

Here's to:
Having money and then losing your jobs
To love and loss
To beauty and truth
To escaping your demons just to get taken down
To having no time to having too much time
To strive for productivity but to be unproductive
To leaving light and loving dark
To almost kill yourself but instead go to the secret park
To waking up just to see you are in the dark
To addiction that consumes your soul
To deaths ganging up on you from all angles
To running away just to come back
To going in a circle when you swore you were on a straight path
To the deep talks that will no longer exist
To reaching the end of your life
And at the last minute changing your mind cuz you do see the light
To feeling healthy to living with illness
To hiking a mountain at the cost of your best friend
For the cold walks in winter had more sun than summer
To the sun being life to the moon's temptation
To feeling confident and then losing your ego
To relying on the ones you stopped trusting to save you
To feeling full of green to taking a knife to your heart
To loving everyone and then hating anything that breathes
To the sunrise
And how it stopped being beautiful to me
To meditation bringing me back
To yoga that unifies me

To the strength that tackled me
To playing music and writing my songs
To playing my songs to one who won't exist
To loving fire which fuels your heart
To finding beauty in water which tears you apart
To having control to having no friends
To always be around people to being alone
To leaving this city in search for home
To making myself better but end up making myself worse
To wanting to take on life
But life took on me first
To living in the moment to being a slave to my past
To 2014 you have ended at last

I Need to Escape

My head is spinning
Anxiety is winning
Paranoia is beginning
I need to escape
My thoughts are flying
My heart is crying
My soul is dying
I need to escape
I need to break this pattern of mine
Where I think of the fall
Instead of the climb
One day I'll see the sun
It will pierce through my soul
It will strengthen me
And make me whole
Until I get there
I feel shut down
My family is sick
And doesn't sleep sound
I worry about others
As well as myself
But I'm in no place
To give any help
My head is spinning
Anxiety is winning
Paranoia is beginning
I need to escape
My thoughts are flying
My heart is crying

My soul is dying
I need to escape
I can't sit still
I need to move
I can't stay in one place
There is too much to do
I am so confused
And so upset
My heart sinks deeper
With every step
Oh my heart sinks deeper with every step!
Like a child in the rain
Or an abandoned pet
My bed, my couch, and kitchen too
Hold memories of pain
And memories of truth
The shower, the sink, the sparkles that fly
They hit my skin
And catch my eye
My head is spinning
Anxiety is winning
Paranoia is beginning
I need to escape
My thoughts are flying
My heart is crying
My soul is dying
I need to escape

Orchids

How many times have I tried to break these chains
Each step forward has pulled me back
My heart has been working overtime
While sense of peace I lack
February wore me out
I have nothing left
So many battles within me
Leaving me a mess
I sit at a table
While orchids sing
I look around
And start to think
Illuminated signs
Begin to move
Slowly they take over
This whole room

The Dance of Shadows

Lips you want to bite
Eyes that pierce through your soul
Death is buried in the ground
Or at least that's what I'm told
Pale skin like winter
Each touch velvet like snow
Every time my heart speeds up
Your ice melts and makes it grow
The heat I have within me
Yearns for something cool and calm
You appear as fire in the light
But at night you prove me wrong
I am a shadow of the night
You are the light that projects my shape
The dance of shadows taught me love
Its intangibility taught me hate
My hands searched for a grip
Just something they could hold
Death is a stiff, breathless corpse
Or at least that's what I'm told
Every tear that landed on my cheek
Came from these icicles I call eyes
Each tear holding the dance of shadows
In a watery disguise
My mind contained a box
That was leaking all the time
It leaked of darkness in the moments
The sun refused to shine
You pried the box open

It exploded in my head
Darkness no longer leaked
But now became my bed
I lie in a bed
That feels so dark and cold
Death takes you when the time is right
Or at least that's what I'm told
I thought it was a dance of shadows
That's what it appeared to be
But when I looked closer
The only shadow there was me
We all have a shadow
We tend to hide that side the most
I just wish I had realized
My shadow had danced with a ghost

The Beach

My heart is heavy
I am in pain
I sit at the beach
And hear the train
It started at the lake
With a notebook and a pen
The freedom I once felt
I long to feel again

One year dead is one year too long

Here I sit
Writing with rage
Writing every single word
On every single page
Life has been on replay and I'm tired of this song
I swear one year dead is one year too long!
Constantly walking up
This staircase we call life
Every single step with the sharpness of a knife
Each step brings me closer to a place where I belong
I swear one year dead is one year too long!
Every eye I look at
Is either asleep
Or awake in this life
Living in misery
I never broke my morals
I never did anyone wrong
I swear one year dead is one year too long!
Tired of looking inward
I'm ready to look out
Become a part of this world
I have learned so much about
God told me I was weak
Gave me hard times to make me strong
I swear one year dead is one year too long!
Tired of separating
Myself from this place
Analyzing features
On every single face
I wasn't always cold

Just people did me wrong
So I died for a year but that's one year too long!
Yoga, meditation
Consciousness grows
So I can leave behind this life that I know
Transcending, growing
Moving with the gong
Cuz I swear one year dead is one year too long

By the Pier

My soul longs for my uke
These ripples long for the light
It's not my fault my body
Responds better to the night
Every time I try
I always seem to fall
Can't you see I collapsed?
And I'm sick of it all?
Doubting every smile
Doubting every thought
Doing everything I can
To be in a better spot
Illuminating wheel
Doesn't the lake look pretty?
So convincing of beauty
In such a horrid city

K

My thoughts are the lake on a windy day
This is to the man whose name starts with a 'K'
Overwhelmed with emotion
On this full moon
Taurus is the month
While Scorpio is the tune
Rain falls and hits the ground
Quenching the thirst of this moonlight sound
Heart is flying in my chest
Refusing to steady
Refusing to rest
Compared to you
How unstable I seem
You are the comfort of a mattress
While I'm a broken dream
You care about me
When times are rough
You don't want me to fall
You don't want me to give up
All the nights we talk on the phone
And that time you told me
Not to feel alone
The things I have told you
Have not been pretty
They have been about my struggle
In this cold-hearted city
You listened close
To what I had to say
You convinced me I'd get better and that I'd be ok

How stressed out and burdened I feel
Dealing with my health and trying to heal
I have been through worse
Things have never been alright
But going through health problems
Took my ego's life
How I've been mourning who I once was
But it's time to grow up and be a woman of love
I don't care about degrees and I don't care about wealth
I just care that you loved me
When I couldn't love myself
Strength and wisdom embody you
I know some of your past and what you have been through
With all the things you have told me and more
You were able to take on life and open a new door
How much compassion I have for you
I see what you have done
And I want to do it too
I know there is distance
But I don't even care
We have our own lives
You don't get in my hair
I don't know why I'm writing
I don't know why I feel this way
But things have been different
Ever since it became May
You understand my patterns
You understand my mind
But don't let that confuse you
I'll still surprise you every time
You connect well with others
I am good at doing that too
I can't imagine the connection
When I am once again with you

The rain has stopped falling
As the ground begins to dry
I want you to join me
As I begin to fly

To Amanda

Call me a bookshelf
That is what I have become
I remain still
There is no need to run
Books are placed upon me
I am used to it now
Each book containing why
Each book containing how
Every story
Every word
Every voice
That was never heard
Every perspective
From every eye
Every nice to meet you
And every goodbye
Every person I meet and get to know
Places a book on me before they go
Some books are light and fairly brief
Others are heavy
Weighted with grief
The books will pile
Until I collapse
I need a strong foundation
So I can last
When the books began
To pile up
I was ready to fall
I was ready to give up

The biggest books
Broke a shelf or two
But I am repaired
And even better than new
The heaviest book I contain is my own
The story of a girl and her search for home
All these books
As well as my own
Rest upon me
Like muscle on bone
The shelf I am can no longer break
To let all these books go
Would be a mistake
As weighted down and burdened as I feel
It's because these books aren't fantasy
They are brutally real
Each book I hold
Contributes to my own
A paperback trail
Leading me home
You see I am not just a body, mind, and soul
I am a bookshelf
Each book making me whole

Decaying Tree

Things are looking up
Maybe even falling into place
But still I'm traumatized and afraid of the future I must face
Terrified of loss and terrified of success
Feel like a decaying tree
With only a few branches left
My roots deep in the earth
How grounded I have become
People don't understand when they tell me I chose to run
All they see is running
To them it is unclear
Ahead of me is a finish line and at last it's becoming near
She washes the dishes and she thinks of him
Escalating smile
When she thinks of what their friendship could have been
She's been growing old
As he is nowhere in sight
It doesn't feel ok
It doesn't feel alright
It's approaching five years now
Convinced herself she has made peace
She has moved on with her life
Her mourning has decreased
She wishes she held on
Instead of pushing the memories away
Because now it has become harder
To remember the words he had to say
I was listening to musicals
It has been a pretty hard day

For what it's worth
I love you friend
And I trust that wherever you are
That you are ok

Reborn

Finally making peace
Feel the sweet release
Letting go
Of the recent past that followed me
I thought I was free from my past
Until a new one formed
A cycle I thought had died
Had only been reborn

To the Sunrise

To the sunrise
And how it once again became beautiful to me
So to everyone I love
I wish you well on your journey
Just something I have learned
Is the best ones are never pretty
They are filled with pain, depression, and cruelty
But you can get through it
Just please stay with me
I'm climbing to the top
So please climb along with me
I swear no one can comprehend
This beauty that is always with me
Through whatever I go through
And whatever I face
I'm never gonna let anything
Take me out of this place
To the beauty that killed me
I'm sorry to you I grew weak
You became everything I look at
And every word I speak
Everything I touch
And everything I feel
Every chance to bruise
And every chance to heal
To the enlightenment
I finally reached
Thank you for being
Available to me

Thank you God
I know you are there
Thanks to everyone who loves
Thanks to everyone who cares

In love with Time

Mondays I do yoga
While on Tuesdays I drink wine
The man who swears he loves me
Is really in love with time
Sitting on a train
Together we sit alone
No one caring for the ride
All just caring to get home
Cracking knuckles next to me
Conversation up ahead
My life turned green after a year of being red
Look at what's around you
Try to read it if you can
Time, you don't have me fooled
I know it's you who has my man
Possession depression
Time making selection
No ending to questions
Why question at all
Answers like dancers
Around in a spiral
When after a while
It's time where they fall
Possession is depression
Cuz you make the selection
To claim something as yours and then hand it to time
They think I look fine and I do look fine
But every passing second only takes what was mine
Arm around her waist

Facebook on his phone
Everything I see is a time given loan
Dream catcher earrings
Seduction by the door
You think you have the answer
But are you really sure?
I think of my friends as I let out a sigh
I swear to god I won't lose another to July
So you threaten a woman
Cuz you think you are a man
Taking away her safety
Threatening her plans
So you can back off and you wanna know why?
I already swore I won't lose another to July
So to the heated weather and to all the violent crimes
I not only blame people but I also blame time
Maybe things work out and the sun always shines
But the man who swears he loves me
Is really in love with time

Vegas and Love

I wrote of lost love
It's a very painful fact
So if anyone cares
If anyone follows
I am finally saying I gained it back
I dream of you every night
When I wake up I need to see your face
I had my doubts about us
But my heart was in a protected place
Stained glass emotions
I didn't expect to feel this way so soon
Every time I'm with you
I feel like my heart is with the moon
Something was off with us
There was a missing piece
I found it once you smiled
And once I saw your teeth

Another Try

Time is not all there is
Yet it's behind every door
I thought I'd find my destiny
But now I'm not even sure
What I love is dying on me and I can't let it go
I have to take my power back and that is all I know
Every time something is wrong
The blame gets put on me
Learning that love is what I want
But respect is what I need
Take these handprints
Savor them
And then let them go
If you hold on to hands for life
How can you expect to grow?
I gave my life away to him and I will never regret it
I gave it away to take it back and I can't let myself forget it

Watching someone be happy without you

Pain is watching someone be happy without you
Pain is watching someone die without you
Pain is watching someone be happy without you
But you hear it in his voice that he's barely hanging on
Or you hear it in his voice that he gave up writing songs
Or you hear it in his voice
He had control all along
Pain is watching
Watching this world
Watching the people
How they come together magnetically just to get torn apart
They come together gracefully just to have a broken heart
They come together willfully cuz they found another part
They begin to form community they yearn for a new start
The pieces come together til they form a piece of art
You hang it on your wall and then people throw their darts
If you happen to get hit then you weren't being smart
Pain is listening
Listening to this piano tune as life goes up and down
Listening to

The empty air

And the peace it found
Listening to the peace that's absent when I'm not around
You claim to have this peace and you claim your life is on track
I'll go to bed at night and pray that one day you will want me back
Knocked over once again
I know this pain all too well

I know I'll rise above it
I refuse to return to hell
Maybe one day we will talk
Look back at this and laugh
Joke about what you did to me and how you claimed to be my
path
Joke about your stability and how it wasn't there
Or how you kicked me out when I ran out of things to share
Joke about how through all of this I know you loved and cared
But your love was limited and that's what wasn't fair
Pain is broken promises and manipulated words
Pain is sinking low when we should be up there with the birds
Pain is your actions never matching what I heard
Pain is I'm the one who left
But you pushed me to that point
Pain is sitting separately when you and I are joint
Pain is feeling
Feeling the wind hit your face and it's too powerful and cold
Or when you look at life and it feels routine and old
Or subconsciously pushing yourself to fit society's mold
I was told that pain is suffering
I was told beauty is shaped on pain
But beauty is when someone gives me shelter in the rain
Beauty is when someone doesn't let me go down the drain
Beauty is when someone doesn't let me get on that plane
Beauty is when opposites realize they are the same
Pain is watching beauty
Watching it
Fade
Away

Gold

Your skin glitters in gold
Your eyes are the sun
From the moment that you smiled
I knew you were the one
I don't understand
Your and my relation
I guess that in order to heal
Sometimes we need separation

People call me the sun

Here I sit
Alone
Here I sit
Ok
Sometimes I feel misled like I was led astray
Been drinking so much wine
Convinced myself I'm fine
Convinced myself I shine
Convinced myself I shine
I should have meditated
I could have cleared my head
I sit here thinking of
All the words I said
Maybe this journey is a pit
Or a portal that sucks my soul
Just
Know I won't let go
No I won't let go
No I won't let go
So I will keep to myself and I'll stay out of your way
When I packed my bags
You had nothing to say
I am so let down
Isn't it a shame?
They would call me the sun
But to you
The sun doesn't faze you in any way
Here I sit
Frustrated

Here I sit
With stress
Sometimes I feel depleted rather than at my best
Just wanna enjoy my life
But it is one big test
It is one big test
It is one big test
I need to do some yoga and connect with earth
It's hard to get things done
It all feels like work
Maybe this journey is a pit
Or a portal that sucks my soul
Just
Know I won't let go
No I won't let go
No I won't let go
So I will keep to myself and I'll stay out of your way
When I packed my bags
You had nothing to say
I am so let down
Isn't it a shame?
They would call me the sun
But to you
The sun doesn't faze you in any way

Go back

I miss how lighthearted I once was
When I was just a girl
Not a woman of love
The moon was my companion
Music guided my path
So many times
I just wish to go back

Sitting in the secret park

Sitting in the secret park
On a warm November night
Those who run through my mind
Get my attention and my sight
Growing frustrated
I wasn't supposed to sit here so soon!
I look up to the sky
But I do not see the moon
Missing desert breeze and the basketball games at night
Missing my bed
Missing my appetite
I was given zero chances
But I gave him as many chances I could lend
Hoping the good I put into the universe
Comes back to me in the end

Left me to your dirt

You were my companion
You were my best friend
I sit here without you
Is this really how you wanted things to end?
Do you understand what you did to me?
Is it that hard to give an apology?
I thought so highly of you
I gave you all the love I had inside
You told me great things
But now I see you lied
Consider myself fooled
Consider myself tricked
I thought you were sincere
Which was why you were the one I picked
I sit next to orchids
As darkness envelops the sky
I'm sorry I'm not effortless and wanted you to try!
So much effort it was for you!
To stand there with a pen!
Checking the boxes off your list that could qualify our end!
You watched me as I struggled
You sat back while I worked
You handed me your shovel
And left me to your dirt
Thank you for coming into my life and deciding to care about me
I hope one day you learn how to take responsibility
I have no hard feelings
I wish the best for you
I hope your life will match
That pretty picture that you drew

Love is enough

Sitting in the purple
Looking at the damage that was done
Tears fall from my eyes
When I think of what we have become
Life with him seemed so real
For once there was something I could hold
But then one too many times
He left me in the cold
He would appear
Then disappear
He had mastered the magician's path
Then one day we got drunk and I realized his wrath
I felt defeated and afraid
But know,
I lost the battle
Not the war
Decided many years ago
That love is worth fighting for

How it all began

I sit at the lake with paper
This is how it all began
Jumped in the lake
Realized it was my soul
And through this lake I swam
At first the waters were calm
The sun shined like how it shines today
Grew tired of the surface
Decided to sink
But then the sun went away
Directionless and without sight
I became afraid
Then began to analyze
Every decision I had made
Stuck in the waters
Couldn't engage with a life I had once known
Didn't know where I was going
Just knew I wanted to find home
Deeper and deeper
There was no going back
Enveloped in these waters
I had never felt so trapped
This wasn't what I expected
On this journey through my soul
I thought I would be free
But instead was swallowed whole
Lost faith in the waters
I had never felt so tricked
Decided to rely on myself and my ability to predict

Predictions turned to fear
For these waters were too rough
My heart was bleeding
My mind was screaming
That I had enough
I opened up my eyes and looked at the life around
Comfort ran through me
When my feet finally hit the ground

Chaos

You are the microscopic knives
That my blood carries through my veins
You are the absence that occurs
When I stand alone in the rain
I will stand in a carless street
And still get hit by your train
You are the knife that I wake up to
When I thought it was safe enough to sleep
You are the cloudless sky
When I'm stuck in the desert heat
You are the smile that makes the world stop
Or at least the world that I used to know
You are the impatience in my spirit
That decided it was time for me to grow
You are the eyes that see so clear
But where is your balance to catch your fall?
You freely give chaos to my life
And leave me to deal with it all
You carried the significance of community
But with the romance of the wise
You are the lightening I got struck by
And then I pretended to be surprised

The World

I am within souls
In cement
The world out there
Is creating all these arguments
So much champagne to the new life you worked for and how it is
a minute walk from home
Right now
I'm in the process of moving into the new year
That will be more productive and less harmful
It is a lot to walk all the time
And leave the anger
Make or break my situation with time painting over
It will be one that succeeds
We can figure it out
Once he is out
Then I'll head that way
To a more productive and less harmful place
When in prison it takes a lot to catch up with time
It's most likely a soundtrack
The tea party of my anxiety
Finding out the feelings don't just go
Went to the prison
Went to cement
We can figure it out
Once he is out
The new year is more productive and less harmful
Time is painting over
He is out of the car and is doing something to my mind
My gut instinct is to work for the people who give to me

They give to get anything
I have the rest of the world
It's better to put me in the spiritual place
It's a good soundtrack
The prison is saying
I was scared of my anxiety
You love me
I open up to you like this is the last night of my life
I remember you are interested
My mind and my heart don't know how to get my mind out of this
The emotion is so bad
I'm scared they have given to me to get anything
The world is better to me than to put me in pain

You are the sun

You came into my life so I could watch you fade away
I see you are the sun
You sought me out
Brought my insanity to light
Once I was aware
Then you were done
I watch the clouds move over you
They cover you quite well
Do you know you are the reason?
That there is light in hell?

You and Water

What I am about to write is not easy
But it is time
It may be cold
But I can still feel the sun shine
Oh it would be nice
To sometime see you again
But there is a chance I won't
And this is the end
I sit at the lake and I watch it move
There is something about water
That will always remind me of you
Whatever you are looking for
I hope it is something you find
It hurts you search without me
But from the start
I knew you were not "mine"
You gave me light when I was locked in the dark
I will never forget that
But that is no longer my start
Today is the day
I start brand new
And can no longer be haunted
By the disappearance of you
I can't even be mad
There is no reason to shout
At the end of the day
I know what you're about
With me
Things are real

You were unable to hide
I know that is a reason
You chose to leave my side
I let you go
So go be free
And when the rain touches your skin
I hope you think of me

The Scarf

Don't call anything your everything
Don't get too attached
Once it's there it could be
Gone in a flash
What happens then?
If your everything is gone?
Will you walk the right way?
Or is it all wrong?
Will you sit by the lake?
Gazing at the sun?
Or will you hide yourself away?
Until the light is done?
Will you sit alone?
Crying in a room?
Or will you sit outside?
Under the moon?
The choice is yours
Do whatever it is that you want
It took me too many years
To realize what I've got

Passing by

I met him while I was walking
I was simply passing by
I was walking thru the desert
And then he caught my eye
He noticed the bag I carried
He showed me he had one too
He escorted me on my way
And promised to help me through

Someone took a bat
They hit me several times
My heart shattering within me
But stronger than ever was my mind
Mental chaos around me
It showed me the way my mind can be used
I began to train my mind
He showed me he had done that too

How cruel the world seemed
In refuge I took the power of my mind
There was so much for me to explore
There was so much for me to find
I picked up all the pieces
I explored every clue
I analyzed myself
He showed me he had done that too

The phone substituted my mattress
It was the best way to fall asleep

It wasn't often I could talk about
How secretly I lurk deep
I exposed my sinking nature
That I was past where the ocean was blue
He removed the veil
And showed me he was lurking there too

The sun came out for me
A new start had begun
I was ready to engage
I was ready to have fun
I ran back to the desert
Ready to start brand new
He showed me he was ready
He showed me he wanted that too

We walked together in the desert
With our bags on our backs
I began my journey
And hoped to never look back
As we were walking
He noticed a mistake
His bag was too heavy
So he gave me all his weight

Just Not Now

There will be a time and place for me
But I guess it is just not now
The thread is unraveling
And I don't really know how
Life is always moving
We are dictated by the sun
I remember when he met me
But I didn't know he would be the one
I see everyone moving forward
So tell me why the direction I'm going is down?
I have been losing energy
I am sinking thru the ground
Weighted, heavy, asleep
Beginning to feel the summer heat
Eyelids are closing
Energy is far away
I have been getting angrier at myself everyday
Consumed by always trying to get things done
Trying to be perfect
But it's a hard race to run
Never feel like I do anything right
Been feeling this way
Because of old fights

My Surrender

I sit on a dock
On the other side of Lake Michigan
Look out
See the trees
Look out
Feel the breeze
Surrounded by water
My mind seems to move as fast
Surrounded by spider webs
They are built so strategically
A pattern to catch their prey
They are built so strategically
A pattern for things to go their way
I no longer aspire to fly
For I fly into other's webs
I take off my wings and decide to build a web instead
No more flying away
No more climbing up
This is my surrender
This is how I give up

Montrose

I remember when I couldn't eat
I remember when I couldn't sleep
I chose to leave that life
I chose to walk away
Isn't life a fun game
If you think you are invincible
Isn't life a fun game
If your soul decides to stay
I am pretty

Don't leave me
I am beautiful

Love me

Those are the words I never get a chance to say
I sit at the lake
With the skyline in front of me
I sit at the lake
As the sun goes away
He called me up with anger
But for that I will not judge
I will let him be alone
Until he finds someone easier to love
I once had community and I threw it in the trash
What I saw with that community
Was no potential to last
Tired of shallow friendships
I gave away a tribe

I chose to be alone
I chose to travel and hide
I see the difference in my life
I see where my gut has led me
I am no longer capsized
But I am sailing pretty steadily
The water turns to glass
Into the shards that are my heart
They no longer feel so heavy
But guide me towards my start

Sunrise 2017

To the sunrise
And how the water is what stands out to me
So to everyone I love
I wish you well on your journey
Just something I have learned
Is the best ones are never pretty
They are filled with pain, depression, and cruelty
Some people struggle through it
Some people don't stay with me
With all I have gone through and all I have faced
I have not let anything take me out of this place
To the waves that drowned me
And to the ocean that became my home
They showed me how to swim
And they showed me how to swim alone
All the travels I have gone on
All the people I decided to trust
They all taught me something
I can't thank them all enough
To the future
I finally see
Thank you for giving back to me
Thank you God
And may I use my will to determine my fate
Thanks to everyone who stands by me
Thanks to everyone who relates

July

I always die
I die like the seasons
I die like the leaves
How fortunate are leaves to reappear and come back different
than before
I owe all that I am to every closed door
Happiness is in my sight
But it is a tightrope walk away
To approach happiness with tact
Is a trick many do not say
I always die with passion
I always die with a burning heart
I always die in secret
I always die smart
I die to be free
I die to feel whole
But even though I die
What stays alive is my soul
How fortunate am I to reappear and come back different than
before
Many do not know me
Many do not reach my core
Many meet me while I cycle and declare that point to be who I
am
They get let down when I die
They get let down because they don't understand
Doesn't everything turn
Into ruin overtime?
I'm running out of words

I'm running out of rhymes
6 years tomorrow
Marks his death
This is how time works
This is what July does best

Business

Light switch on emotions
I got switched to dark
I really should be studying cuz this class I made a mark
Been doing what I have to
For a future I finally see
I am absorbed in everything
Everything but me
They threw paint at the wall
And I am dripping down
Melting from this college
Until I hit the ground
Walk over to the secret park
Sit down at the lawn
They built so many buildings
That now the sun is gone
October has a chill when you're sitting in the shade
It has been one year and Chicago I have stayed
This year has gone by fast
I had to dig to build
You can call me crazy
Or you can call me skilled
Professors care about me
Friends care about me too
I have gone through hell just so I can be in school
Have an interview soon
And expecting several calls
This is me in the city
This is me in the fall
My life isn't perfect

But I learn to accept
I can't always score 100
I can't always be my best
Things will get me down
But I'll still stick around
Like those trees over there
I am rooted in the ground
Melting like the paint
The rain begins to pour
The only thing between us is a closed glass door
This year has gone by fast
My spirit was almost killed
You can call me crazy
Or you can call me skilled
A sense of community
I know I have lost
Holidays and parties
Are memories that got tossed
I was happy breaking free
But somehow I still crashed
Why does my mind like to linger in the past?
Working to be free
Cuz I have to undo this knot
Cuz whenever I moved forward
It always had me caught
I feel like a ghost
Like my life went on pause
Look at what I've gone through
I bet you'll name a cause
Things aren't so bad
I don't mean to get so sad
There's just pain in my stomach
That I wish I never had

This year has gone by fast
But the cup I threw got filled
You can call me crazy
Or you can call me skilled

Hollow Soul

A tree decaying within
I am a hollow soul
His music plays when I close my eyes
His presence lingers by my side
I walked within the shadows
Now he is the shadow that walks within me
A locked door was my obstacle
While his obstacle was the key
In shock and with a clouded mind
In the heart of the city alone
I called in case his presence died
But his presence answered the phone
I lay nearly dead myself
No one knows my lips went dry
My skins been losing color
I no longer cry
I don't know if I can take it anymore
I don't know how to express the pain
I am always occupied
I am always drained
Attribute meaning to me
I am the light bulb that burned out
I am the sand that's in the desert
The sand everyone forgets about
Chaos all around me
Chaos in my head
A murderer went to Vegas
And now 59 are dead
Memories on the strip

Memories at Mandalay
Are now tainted by videos
Of watching where the bodies lay
That was once my home
Each bullet hits my mind
That wasn't supposed to happen
That wasn't supposed to be their time
Goodbye to the dollar jello shots
Goodbye to the shows
This is what people do
This is how violence goes
You find a pretty city
You have yourself a good time
The memories turn to darkness
Once someone commits a crime

Hands of the Clock

I can take a breath
The hands of the clock are knives
Every minute stabs me
Every hour makes me wise
Time is running out
I try to catch the sand
I don't have an exact goal
But I clearly have a plan
What powers the city isn't a current
You can't find it in a wire
Every person goes downtown and gives the city their fire
He welcomes me to broken pieces
He welcomes me to ash
He cleared me from his life
Now he wants me to come back
He places a brick down
Over the memories he killed
But if he really wanted me
A whole house he needs to build
The universe heard me scream
It witnessed my deepest pain
I have lived a life of insanity
But people describe me as sane
I traveled through the seasons
I will travel through some more
It was a difficult journey
And a difficult climb
But now I'm stronger than before

Undo the picture

Most of my life is a song for the past
Chicago, I'm gonna try
I'm bringing my life back home
I'm gonna celebrate now
So have a good night
See if you can get in my head
I think I'm going to be there a lot
Time is out of control
Most of my life
Has been time I was not with him
I'll head over to the beach
It is the closest thing to make me feel good
The lake is worth it
I did not get back on my own time
My way home is different
I was trying to make the situation go away
I was trying to undo the picture

Breakdown

My eyes are filled with tears
My heart feels like it's going to burst
Appearing to be the best impact
You turned out to be the worst
Distracting myself from memories
Your name has been erased from my phone
There's no one I could talk to about it
So this past year I struggled alone
The pain began as heavy
Then morphed itself to sharp
I can't predict its end
Because I can't pin point its start
There are words I never said because I didn't want to come
across too strong
I'm in a better spot now
But I think it took me too long
It's a rush when you are suffering
And one person gives love to you
And when that same person kicks you out
You feel a certain way too
It is pain I cannot shake
It finds me in the night
It has been a while so I guess it takes more than time to feel
alright
I have been through so much change I can't recognize my
reflection
All this pain coming from a person with whom I have a deep
connection
I had to suck up my emotions

To work hard and get through the day
But by doing this
I just drank my pain away
This is coming from retrospect
This poem isn't swayed
I can't even be mad
Considering all the progress I have made
Sometimes I cry when I should be doing work for school
It's not the pain of loss
But of feeling like I was fooled
The problem was I trusted
That voice that sent me to sleep
I trusted that voice to the point
I trust my own heartbeat
This is pain I never anticipated
These are weights I never wanted
Even the people I talk to
Can tell that I feel haunted
I'm not trying to invade
I'm not trying to take the floor
I just have to write this out because I can't hold it in anymore
Your logic is complex
Your spontaneity is quite stunning
I can sometimes see the future
And I never saw that coming
I've only known you a few years
But that doesn't seem quite right
Because the weapon that you stabbed me with
Has stabbed me my whole life
What's strange is when you kicked me out and you closed and
locked the door
I went swimming in your mental waves just trying to explore
You can call that kindness

Or you can call that compassion
I know my exploration
Gives me a delayed reaction
It's almost like this was your method
It's almost like this was your plan
You're the one who hurt me
But you're also the one who understands
I don't have a dramatic end for this
This isn't trying to get across a theme
This is just my experience
With someone I once shared dreams

She Grew

He brought me to life just to kill me again
Before him
I did not die enough
I have become tired
From being replanted
And growing where hearts are rough
I know what he had done to me
I know what he put me through
He will wait another couple years
And tell himself "she grew"
He sees me as inferior
He speaks to me as if I am a kid
He doesn't understand me
And he honestly never did
Too many bad things happened to me
I told him about this place
He continued to manipulate me
So I told him I need space
I went from being "the one"
To being "not ideal"
I learned the difference of a con and of something that is real
There was never something I could truly hold
The icicle melted
And now I'm just cold
He was someone I was in love with
He even began as a friend
But his love was a game
And the game reached its end